KICK, JUMP, CHEER!

CHEERLEADING PROFESSIONALS

BY SARA GREEN

BELLWETHER MEDIA • MINNEAPOLIS, MN

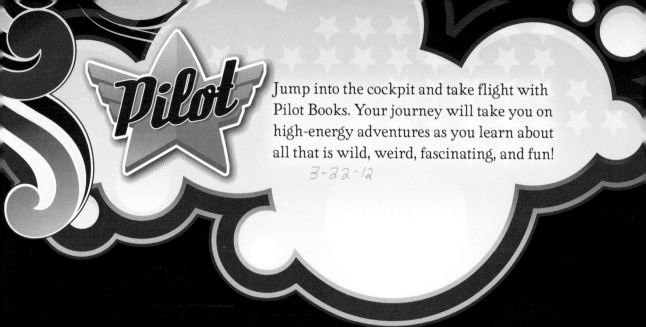

Jump into the cockpit and take flight with Pilot Books. Your journey will take you on high-energy adventures as you learn about all that is wild, weird, fascinating, and fun!

3-22-12

This edition first published in 2012 by Bellwether Media, Inc.

No part of this publication may be reproduced in whole or in part without written permission of the publisher.
For information regarding permission, write to Bellwether Media, Inc.,
Attention: Permissions Department,
5357 Penn Avenue South, Minneapolis, MN 55419.

Library of Congress Cataloging-in-Publication Data
Green, Sara, 1964–
 Cheerleading professionals / by Sara Green.
    p. cm. — (Pilot books: kick, jump, cheer!)
 Includes bibliographical references and index.
 Summary: "Engaging images accompany information about cheerleading professionals. The combination of high-interest subject matter and narrative text is intended for students in grades 3 through 7"—Provided by publisher.
 ISBN 978-1-60014-649-7 (hardcover : alk. paper)
 1. Cheerleading—Juvenile literature. I. Title.
 LB3635.G744 2011
 791.6'4—dc22   2011010382

Printed in the United States of America, North Mankato, MN.

080111   1187

CONTENTS

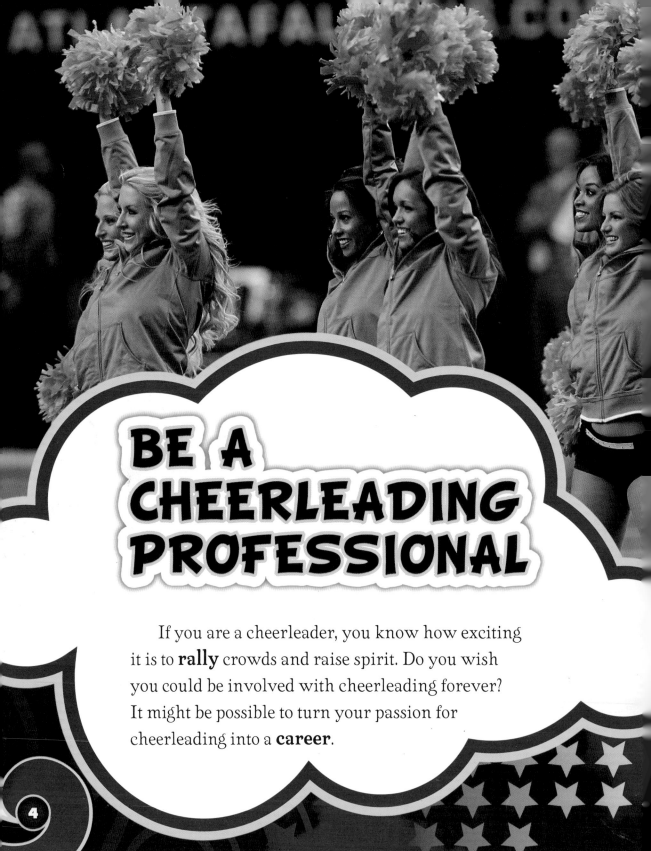

BE A CHEERLEADING PROFESSIONAL

If you are a cheerleader, you know how exciting it is to **rally** crowds and raise spirit. Do you wish you could be involved with cheerleading forever? It might be possible to turn your passion for cheerleading into a **career**.

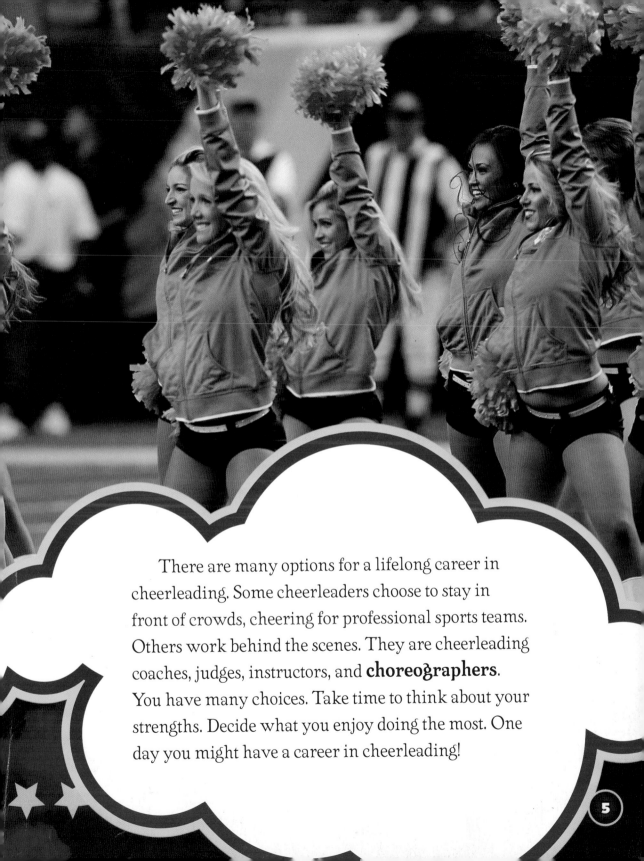

There are many options for a lifelong career in cheerleading. Some cheerleaders choose to stay in front of crowds, cheering for professional sports teams. Others work behind the scenes. They are cheerleading coaches, judges, instructors, and **choreographers**. You have many choices. Take time to think about your strengths. Decide what you enjoy doing the most. One day you might have a career in cheerleading!

PRO SPORTS CHEERLEADERS

It's game day. The stadium is filled with thousands of football fans. A **squad** of professional cheerleaders runs onto the field. They are excited to rev up the crowd with their cheering, dancing, and **tumbling**. Professional cheerleaders perform at football and basketball games. Most professional cheerleaders cheer for teams in the National Football League (NFL) and National Basketball Association (NBA). Squads entertain sports fans during time-outs and other breaks in play. They often perform dance **routines** that include hip hop, jazz, and **kickline** moves. Their spirit fires up the crowd at every game!

The Laker Girls are one of the most famous NBA cheerleading squads. They are known for their athletic, jazzy dance routines.

The Dallas Cowboys Cheerleaders forever changed the way professional cheerleaders performed. In 1972, they were the first squad to perform choreographed dance moves instead of traditional cheers and chants. The crowd loved this new style of cheering.

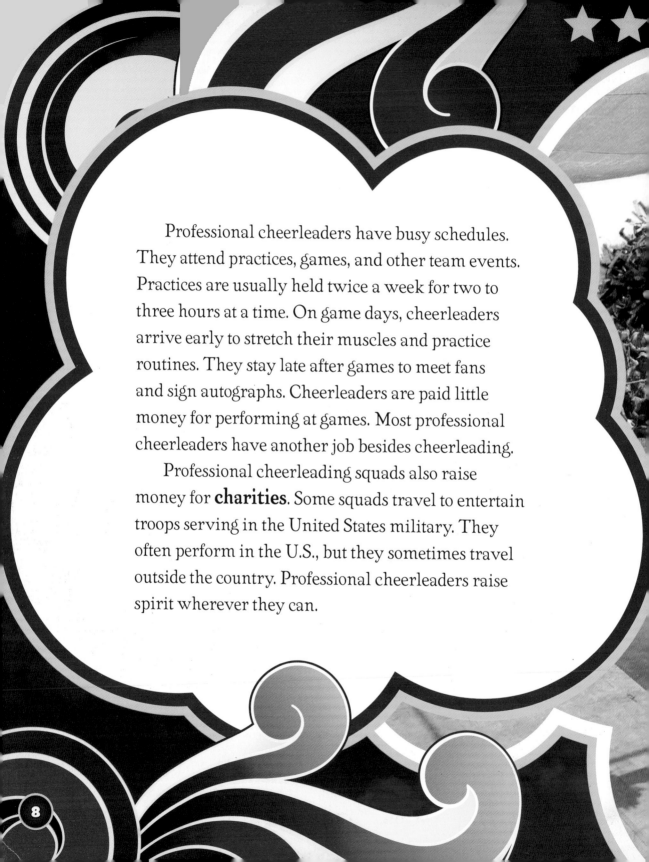

Professional cheerleaders have busy schedules. They attend practices, games, and other team events. Practices are usually held twice a week for two to three hours at a time. On game days, cheerleaders arrive early to stretch their muscles and practice routines. They stay late after games to meet fans and sign autographs. Cheerleaders are paid little money for performing at games. Most professional cheerleaders have another job besides cheerleading.

Professional cheerleading squads also raise money for **charities**. Some squads travel to entertain troops serving in the United States military. They often perform in the U.S., but they sometimes travel outside the country. Professional cheerleaders raise spirit wherever they can.

The Dallas Cowboys Cheerleaders have performed for United States troops in Iraq.

All professional cheerleaders must go through a **tryout**. Competition is tough. Hundreds of cheerleaders show up to the tryout. They must have outstanding **showmanship** and dancing skills to stand out and make the cut. Even returning cheerleaders must try out to keep their spots on a squad!

The tryout has three rounds. In the first round, the whole group performs a dance routine together. The judges pick the best dancers to move on to the second round. In the second round, these dancers perform another routine. Judges look for the cheerleaders with the most spirit and talent. These cheerleaders move on to the final round. In this round, judges interview the finalists to get to know them. Finalists also perform an individual dance. The best cheerleaders are invited to join the squad.

COACHES

Cheerleading routines are exciting and creative. Have you ever wondered how cheerleaders learn so many moves? They have great coaches! It is a big responsibility to be a cheerleading coach. Coaches are leaders, teachers, and role models to cheerleaders of all ages.

Coaches run tryouts, manage practices, teach cheerleading skills, and attend performances. They teach cheerleaders how to practice and perform in a safe way. Coaches **motivate** cheerleaders to set goals and achieve them. They encourage teamwork and **sportsmanship**. Coaches also plan fitness programs. They teach cheerleaders how to improve their **stamina**, strength, and **flexibility**. Great coaches keep cheerleaders on their game and push them to new levels!

JUDGES

Competitions are an important part of cheerleading. At these events, squads compete against each other in front of large crowds. The squad that performs their routine the best wins. Judges have front row seats at competitions. Their scores determine who wins. Most competitions have **performance judges** and **safety judges**. Performance judges sit in front of the stage. They have score sheets and give points for each cheerleading skill that a squad performs. They also write comments about each squad's strengths and weaknesses. Safety judges watch squads closely from the sidelines. They make sure cheerleaders follow the competition rules and stay safe. These judges take away points from squads that break rules.

Most judges are former cheerleaders with a lot of experience. All judges must pass a test to prove they know the names of cheerleading moves and how to do them. They also have to pass a competition test to prove they know how to score the skills.

**PERFORMANCE JUDGES
GIVE POINTS FOR:**
- Squad spirit
- Height of jumps
- Difficulty of stunts and tumbling
- Precision of body movement
- Effective use of music
- Overall performance

**SAFETY JUDGES
TAKE AWAY POINTS FOR:**
- Stepping out of bounds
- Stepping on signs or other props
- Collisions during tumbling moves
- Untied shoelaces
- Poor spotting or too few spotters
- Wearing jewelry

CHOREOGRAPHERS

Someone needs to make cheerleading routines exciting and eye-catching. That person might be you! Choreographers plan routines set to music for professional cheerleaders and competition squads. They combine dance moves, cheerleading skills, and tumbling to create thrilling routines.

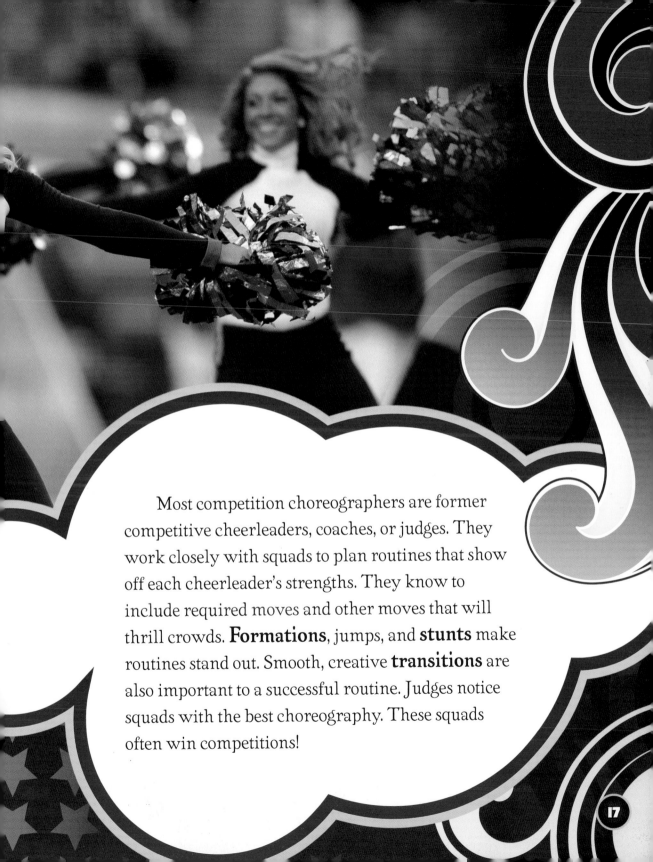

Most competition choreographers are former competitive cheerleaders, coaches, or judges. They work closely with squads to plan routines that show off each cheerleader's strengths. They know to include required moves and other moves that will thrill crowds. **Formations**, jumps, and **stunts** make routines stand out. Smooth, creative **transitions** are also important to a successful routine. Judges notice squads with the best choreography. These squads often win competitions!

CAMP INSTRUCTORS

Many current and former cheerleaders enjoy spending summer working with young cheerleaders. This is what instructors at cheerleading camps get to do! They often teach at several camps during the summer. Some get to travel throughout the country. The best instructors have great dance and tumbling skills. It is also important that they enjoy working with kids.

Camps only hire the best cheerleaders age 18 and older to be instructors. Camp directors often ask the most talented, friendly campers to be instructors when they are old enough. If you have a positive attitude, great cheerleading skills, and a lot of enthusiasm, you might make a great instructor at cheerleading camp!

KEEPING UP WITH CHEERLEADING

Many people dream of a career in cheerleading. Different jobs are available for people who love the sport. There are also other ways to stay involved in cheerleading after high school or college. No matter which path you choose, it's important to keep up with current cheerleading trends. Attend competitions and other events where cheerleaders perform. Talk to coaches about how they learn new skills. Visit a summer cheer camp and seek out the camp directors. They can give you advice about how to become an instructor. If a cheerleading professional has made a difference in your life, you might want to do the same for a young cheerleader. The possibilities are endless in the world of cheerleading!

GLOSSARY

career—work that a person commits to for a long period of time; people advance their careers by gaining knowledge and seeking new challenges in their work.

charities—organizations that help people in need

choreographers—people who plan, arrange, and teach dance steps, cheerleading skills, and tumbling skills

flexibility—the ability to stretch and move the body with ease

formations—eye-catching arrangements of cheerleaders; squads move from one formation to another when performing.

kickline—a formation in which cheerleaders stand in a line and perform high kicks or other moves

motivate—to encourage to do something

performance judges—cheerleading competition judges who give squads scores for different skills

rally—to stir up and encourage enthusiasm

routines—sequences of moves that cheerleaders practice and perform

safety judges—cheerleading competition judges who watch for rule violations

showmanship—the ability to present something in an exciting, engaging way

sportsmanship—showing fair play, respect for others, and grace whether winning or losing

squad—a group of cheerleaders that works together as a team

stamina—the ability to do something for a long time

stunts—cheerleading moves that involve climbing and lifting; in some stunts cheerleaders are thrown into the air.

transitions—changes from one move or formation to other moves or formations

tryout—an event where people perform skills for coaches or judges in order to make a team

tumbling—gymnastics skills such as cartwheels and handsprings; many cheerleading squads use tumbling in their routines.

TO LEARN MORE

At the Library

Coachman, Mary Kaye. *Dance Team*.
New York, N.Y.: Rosen Pub. Group, 2007.

Jones, Jen. *Cheer Professionals: Cheer as a Career*. Mankato, Minn.: Capstone Press, 2008.

Peters, Craig. *Techniques of Dance for Cheerleading*. Philadelphia, Pa.: Mason Crest Publishers, 2003.

On the Web

Learning more about cheerleading is as easy as 1, 2, 3.

1. Go to www.factsurfer.com.

2. Enter "cheerleading" into the search box.

3. Click the "Surf" button and you will see a list of related Web sites.

With factsurfer.com, finding more information is just a click away.

INDEX

The images in this book are reproduced through the courtesy of: Getty Images, front cover, pp. 4-5, 7, 11, 18-19, 21; NBAE/Getty Images, p. 6; Richard Young/Rex USA, p. 9; United States Department of Defense, p. 12; Bloomberg/Getty Images, p. 13; Mike Orazzi/The Bristol Press, p. 15; Jim Mone/AP Images, p. 17.